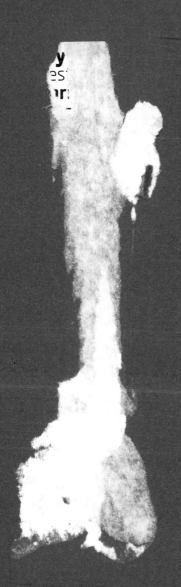

[UNDERSTAND!NG GRAMMAR]

ADJECTIVES *and* PREPOSITIONS

ANN RIGGS

W
FRANKLIN WATTS
LONDON•SYDNEY

First published in the UK in 2012 by
Franklin Watts
338 Euston Road
London NW1 3BH

Franklin Watts Australia
Level 17/207 Kent Street
Sydney, NSW 2000

First published by Creative Education, an imprint of The Creative Company.

A CIP catalogue record for this book is available from the British Library.

ISBN: 978 1 4451 1074 5

Dewey number: 425

Printed in China

Franklin Watts is a division of
Hachette Children's Books,
an Hachette UK company.

www.hachette.co.uk

Design and production by Liddy Walset; Art direction by Rita Marshall

Photographs by Corbis (Heidi Benser, Bowers Museum of Cultural Art), Getty Images
(Peter Cade, Tim Flach, Gone Wild, Hulton Archive, Martin Rogers, Gail Shumway, Kevin Summers,
Kim Taylor, Paul Taylor, David Troncoso, Gandee Vasan), iStockphoto (Kseniya Abramova,
Jill Battaglia, Nick M. Do, Hedda Gjerpen, Andrew Howe, Eric Isselée, Maria Itina,
Jacqueline Kemp, Angelika Schwarz, James Steidl, sumnersgraphicsinc, Tomasz Zacharisz)

Illustrations on pages 30, 31 © 2007 Etienne Delessert

TABLE of CONTENTS

4
INTRODUCTION

CHAPTERS

6
Preferential treatment

14
Limited partnerships

24
Comparing and compounding

32
Just what is a preposition?

40
Significant sidekicks

BUILD YOUR OWN SENTENCE ACTIVITIES

12
Questioning the answer

22
Modifier manoeuvres

30
To infinity and beyond?

38
Lasting relationships

44
Phrasal focus

46
GLOSSARY

47
RESOURCES

48
INDEX

Music swells. Siblings squabble. Owls hoot. I am. Grammar is.

As simply as that, two words can become a SENTENCE. The information in a short sentence can be expanded by adding more words that give vivid descriptions or specific reactions. Where should those words be placed? How does a writer know what PUNCTUATION to use? And what does all of that mean? Words fall into place more easily when one has an understanding of grammar, a system of rules that gives writers the foundation for producing acceptable formal expression. It is that acceptable form, that appropriate grammar, which helps readers comprehend what has been written.

Grab a tennis ball and throw it. That's right – throw it! A probable result is that the ball flies through the air and slams into… something. Or we could say, the ball (a noun) flies (a verb) through (a preposition) the (an article) air (a noun) and (a conjunction) slams (a verb) into (a preposition) the wall, your mate, a plant or a window (all nouns). Each noun could be further described by an adjective. In Latin, *ad-* means 'towards', and *-jacere* means 'throw' and these form the root for the English word 'adjective', which describes characteristics of nouns and their substitutes, pronouns. When you throw an adjective towards a noun, you are hoping it will stick, that it will modify and change the noun into whatever you want it to be, whether that noun is a golf ball, a tennis ball, a rugby ball or a medicine ball that connects with a freshly painted wall, a dozing mate, a flowering plant or perhaps a new window.

Like adjectives, prepositions are also used to describe nouns. But unlike adjectives, prepositions cannot stand on their own as MODIFIERS. Words such as *at*, *by*, *for* and *to* need a noun or pronoun to complete their relationships to the other words in the sentence, as in **The salesman *at* the *door* was persistent.** The prepositional phrase '*at* the door' is related to 'salesman'. However, sometimes prepositions are so firmly *attached to* adjectives in an expression that they almost sound like one word. Wherever they appear in a sentence though, adjectives and prepositions work together to add meaning and value to the sentence as a whole.

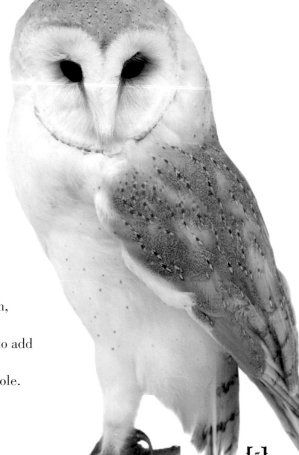

PREFERENTIAL TREATMENT

When you throw a ball do you *lob*, *fling*, *pitch*, *heave*, *launch* or *propel* it? Writers' word choices can enhance or detract from a sentence's meaning and better-written sentences use exact verbs and nouns. How can you find the words that will say what you mean to say? A THESAURUS (in book form or on a computer) is an invaluable resource for locating precise verbs, nouns and modifiers. Adjectives in particular must be carefully chosen, not used simply as fillers in flowery expression.

Where should an adjective be placed? Firstly, identify the nouns and pronouns; then you can look for words to modify them. If you wanted to talk about an animal, for example, what words would you choose to associate with it? Have a look at how Scottish vet and author James Herriot (1916–95) handles this in the following excerpt from the semi-autobiographical novel *The Lord God Made Them All* (1981). Try to identify the nouns (the people, places and things), and then look for the adjectives Herriot uses to describe an incident involving a dog with a chicken bone caught in its mouth. Also watch for Herriot's five-year-old son Jimmy's reaction.

The little man [Mr Anderson], lips tight, eyes like slits, bent and extended trembling hands towards his dog [Venus] but each time he touched her she slithered away from him until, with a great shuddering sigh, she flopped face-down on the tiles [floor]. Jimmy giggled. Things were looking up.

I helped the barber to his feet. 'I'll tell you what, Mr Anderson, I'll give her a

short-acting anaesthetic... Just leave her to me and come back for her in about an hour.'... I slid the needle into the vein... and within seconds her fighting pose relaxed... 'No trouble now, Jimmy, lad,' I said. I pushed the teeth apart effortlessly with finger and thumb, gripped the bone with the forceps and lifted it from the mouth... 'All done.'

My son nodded briefly. Events had gone dull again. He had been hoping for great things when Mr Anderson draped himself along the surgery floor but this was tame stuff. He had stopped smiling.

My own satisfied smile too, had become a little fixed. I was watching Venus carefully, and she wasn't breathing... Jimmy was watching me just as keenly...

He never knew when his father might do

something funny or something funny might happen to
him... His hunch was proved right when I suddenly lifted
Venus from the table... then set off at full gallop... I could
hear the eager shuffle of the little slippers just behind me.

I threw open the side door and shot into the back
garden... and continued my headlong rush till I reached the
big lawn... Oh, this just couldn't happen! I seized Venus by
a hind leg in either hand and began to whirl her round
and round my head. Sometimes higher,
sometimes lower, but attaining a
remarkable speed as I put all my
strength into the swing. This
method of resuscitation seems
to have gone out of fashion now
but it was very much in vogue then. It
certainly met with the full approval of my son.
He laughed so much that he fell down and sprawled
on the grass... And he didn't have to wait more than a
few seconds before Daddy was in full action once more,
with Venus swooping through the air like a bird on the
wing... I don't know how many times I stopped, dropped
the inert form on the grass, then recommenced my
whirling, but at last, at one of the intervals, the chest wall
gave a heave and the eyes blinked... Venus began to lick
her lips and look around her.

,,

One question adjectives answer about nouns and pronouns is *what kind?* Without the modifiers *little*, *tight*, *trembling*, *great* and *shuddering* in the first sentence, we would not be able to tell what kind of reaction Mr Anderson has to his dog's distress. And in the second paragraph we find the answers to *what kind?* of anaesthetic (*short-acting*), Venus's

that not only the descriptions but also the action is picking up! The remaining *what kind?* adjectives include '*hind* leg', '*remarkable* speed', '*full* approval', '*full* action', '*inert* form' and '*chest* wall' to end the account. It's a rather exhausting excerpt but we wouldn't have wanted to miss it, especially the way the author describes it.

Other questions adjectives answer are

WHAT KIND?

pose (*fighting*) and the resulting trouble (*no*). Do you see how the adjectives are tied to the nouns that they describe? Let's look at the third paragraph for more *what kind?* answers: '*great* things', '*surgery* floor' and '*tame* stuff'. Herriot's smile goes from *satisfied* to *fixed* and the fun begins – something *funny* even, describing the '*full* gallop' and Jimmy's '*eager* shuffle' and '*little* slippers'. In paragraph five, by the time, as Mr Herriot says, he **threw open the *side* door and shot into the *back* garden… and continued my *headlong* rush till I reached the *big* lawn,** readers are well aware

how many? and *which?* Often the answer to *how many?* is a number and *which?* signals a specific item or characteristic (*that pink* one). American novelist Frank Norris (1870–1902) reinforces the power of vivid description in his account of the conflict between farmers and railway executives in *The Octopus: A California Story* (1901). In the following excerpt, he describes what it took to get the soil ready for planting. What adjectives does Norris employ to let us know *how many* and *which*?

" The ploughs, thirty-five in number, each drawn by its team of ten, stretched in an interminable [never-ending] line, nearly a quarter of a mile in length... A prolonged movement rippled from team to team, disengaging in its passage a multitude of sounds – the click of buckles, the creak of straining leather, the subdued clash of machinery, the cracking of whips, the deep breathing of nearly four hundred horses, the abrupt commands and cries of the drivers and, last of all, the prolonged, soothing murmur of the thick brown earth turning steadily from the multitude of advancing shears. "

Can you visualise all the horses and hear the drivers? *How many* horses? Nearly 400. *Which* drivers? Theirs. *What kind* of commands? Abrupt. Precise modifiers, such as the numbers 35, 10, one-quarter and 400, team with action verbs (*stretched*, *rippled*) and exact nouns that sound like what they mean: *click*, *creak*, *clash*, *cracking*, *murmur*. Such a combination of details helps give a clear and accurate picture of the scene.

The effectiveness of adjectives and their team-mates, nouns and pronouns, is enhanced by vivid verbs and specific subjects. However, over-using some adjectives is something that can make them meaningless. As much as possible, avoid using *nice*, *good*, *bad*, *funny*, *amazing*, *great* and *fine*. Although it seems like a *nice* day, call it *pleasant*, *sunny*, *cloudless* or *balmy*. A teacher may have worn a *funny* shirt but just label it *unusual* unless it really was *comical*. If you read a *good* book, how good was it? Was it *satisfactory* or *exceptional*? Perhaps it was *entertaining* or merely *brief*. If you feel *fine* about the latest piece of homework you handed in, your teacher may think it's merely *passable*, not *spectacular*. Your definition of *fine* – and any other over-used adjectives – may not match the CONNOTATION. Be vigilant and carry a large rubber. Keep the rubber handy for *thrilled*, *lovely*, *interesting* and *brilliant*. You could just as easily say *entranced*, *whimsical*, *fascinating* or *dazzling*!

NICE GOOD BAD FUNNY AMAZING GREAT FINE CUTE THRILLED WONDERFUL

BUILD YOUR OWN SENTENCE
Questioning the answer

Picture yourself standing in front of the cages at an animal shelter. You've come to choose a pet, to take home one animal that needs your care. The answer is right there in front of you but the questions of *which?* and *what kind?* baffle you. Write a paragraph about the dogs and cats you see there; describe their size and breed, their sounds, their searching eyes. Describe how you feel about being the one person to meet the needs of just one of them. Be sure your complete sentences have accurate adjectives to modify their nouns and pronouns. Without using worn-out words such as 'nice', 'good', 'lovely' and 'amazing', conclude by explaining why you chose the pet you did.

LIMITED PARTNERSHIPS

Because adjectives are connected to the nouns they modify, they can also be classified (like nouns) as COMMON or PROPER. Nations, regions and religions are all proper nouns that can be described as proper adjectives as well: an *African* country, a *Canadian* province and a *Protestant* church. Such adjectives are not limited to describing just one country, province or church, but the use of a proper adjective does narrow our choices. Sometimes a proper adjective and a noun combine to name one particular object that is in itself a noun. Have a look at these everyday items: Cheddar cheese, Italian dressing, Belgian chocolate, French bread.

Each is a noun that uses a proper adjective as part of its name.

Adjectives can work just as easily with verbs to form participial adjectives. A participle is a word formed from a verb. Present participles are formed with a verb and *-ing*, making words such as 'laughing', 'sleeping' and 'sneaking'; past participles are made by combining the main verb with *-ed*, resulting in words such as 'endangered' and 'finished' – or by using an IRREGULAR FORM, as in 'spoken' (speak, spoke, spoken). To make a participial adjective, we join a participle to a noun: a *laughing* hyena, a *sleeping* bag, a *sneaking* suspicion or an *endangered* species; a *finished* product or a *spoken* version. All of these modifiers came from verbs. All of them now describe nouns. Each is a participial adjective.

See how many adjectives – participial or otherwise – you can find in the following excerpt from American author James Fenimore Cooper's (1789–1851) novel *The Last of the Mohicans: A Narrative of 1757* (1826). The white woodsman Hawk-eye along with surviving Mohicans Chingachgook, his son Uncas and the well-meaning Major Duncan Heyward are on a mission to rescue two white women who have been taken captive. Just before the excerpt that follows, they encounter an enemy warrior who takes a shot at Chingachgook. After Uncas follows and kills the man, Heyward is surprised by the Mohicans' reaction to the event.

" Chingachgook turned a calm and incurious eye toward the place where the [rifle] ball had struck, and then resumed his former attitude, with a composure that could not be disturbed by so trifling an incident. Just then Uncas glided into the circle and seated himself at the fire, with the same appearance of indifference as was maintained by his father.

Of these several movements Heyward was a deeply interested and wondering observer. It appeared to him as though the foresters had some secret means of intelligence which had escaped the vigilance of his own faculties. In place of that eager and garrulous [talkative] narration with which a white youth would have endeavoured to communicate, and perhaps exaggerate, that which had passed out in the darkness of the plain, the young warrior was seemingly content to let his deeds speak for themselves. "

Not all the -ed and -ing words you encountered here were participial adjectives – most were really verbs. And in their midst were 15 adjectives: *calm, incurious, former, trifling, same, several, interested, wondering, secret, own, eager, garrulous, white, young, content*. Of these, three were present and past participle modifiers: 'so *trifling* an incident', 'a deeply *interested* and *wondering* observer'. If Cooper had not used *trifling*, signifying the Mohican's understated reaction to what most people would consider a startling event – almost being killed – the reader might have lost the author's sense of subtlety. Simply saying the chief 'didn't appear bothered' takes all the fire out of the explanation. When Major Heyward realises what has happened, both his knowledge of the frontier and his admiration for the Mohicans are enhanced.

Adjectives that help limit the nouns that follow them are called articles. The words *a*, *an* and *the* are articles and are also known as determiners. They point to people, places and things. An article might be used with other adjectives and is usually the first word in a NOUN PHRASE. It indicates something specific and definite (*the* striped shirt) or general and indefinite (*a* clean shirt, *an* endangered animal). When an article is called for, *the* is used with proper nouns, which are specific places, people or things: the River Thames, the Grand Canyon, the Bolton Wanderers, the Churchills, the British Museum or the

Coventry Daily News.

Choosing *a* or *an* for a general, indefinite reference depends on the sound of the word that comes next. Use *a* before singular count nouns (things that can be counted and can have both singular and plural forms) that begin with a consonant sound, including /y/, /h/ and /w/, no matter how the word is spelt: *a* uniform, *a* European, *a* history test, *a* once-in-a-lifetime holiday. Use *an* before singular count nouns that begin with vowels (a, e, i, o, u) or vowel-like sounds, as in *an* apple, *an* honour, *an* uncle, *an* X-ray, *an* MI5 agent. (The abbreviation for the Military Intelligence section 5 – MI5 – is not pronounced with an

m-sound, /m/, but is given the name of the letter *m*, /*em*/, a vowel sound, so the article *an* is correct.) As usage is determined by pronunciation and not spelling, many words that begin with the letter *u* are affected by the /*yoō*/ or the /ə/ sounds. Compare these /*yoō*/ phrases – *a* **UK citizen**, *a* **utilitarian vehicle**

PREDICATE) separated: 'The climb up the mainmast' and 'was torture'. The predicate adjective (*torture*) follows a LINKING VERB (*was*) and modifies the noun subject (*climb*). When there is a describing word after a non-action verb, it could be a predicate adjective. To know for certain, check to see if the descriptor refers to the subject.

The True Confessions of Charlotte Doyle (1990), written by American author Avi (1937–), recounts the voyage of a 13-year-old girl in

THE MI5

and *a* **unilateral decision** – with these /ə/ phrases: *an* **understanding employer**, *an* **uppercase letter** and *an* **unmistakable resemblance**.

An article always appears near the noun or pronoun it describes. But sometimes adjectives are positioned further from the words they modify. When an adjective is found in the predicate, the part of the sentence that contains the verb, it is known as a predicate adjective. The following sentence has its two parts (COMPLETE SUBJECT and COMPLETE

an 1832 Atlantic Ocean crossing. Charlotte's courage and stamina are put to the ultimate test when she must climb the 40-metre-tall mainmast. Can you find the 27 adjectives that add drama to the following scene? Included are eight predicate adjectives.

"This final climb was torture. With every upward pull the swaying of the ship seemed to increase. Even when not moving myself, I was flying through the air in wild, wide gyrations. The horizon kept shifting, tilting, dropping. I was increasingly dizzy, nauseous, terrified, certain that with every next moment I would slip and fall to death. I paused again and again, my eyes on the rigging inches from my face, gasping and praying as I had never prayed before... But then at last with trembling fingers, I touched the spar of the royal yard [the horizontal pole beneath the topmost sail]. I had reached the top.

Once there I endeavored to rest again. But there the metronome motion of the mast was at its most extreme, the *Seahawk* turning, tossing, swaying as if trying to shake me off – like a dog throwing droplets of water from its back. And when I looked beyond I saw a sea that was infinity itself, ready, eager to swallow me whole."

SHIFTING TILTING DROPPING DIZZY NAUSEOUS TERRIFIED CERTAIN

Locating the linking verbs *was* and *kept* (past tense of *keep*), which occur after their subjects, helps us identify modifiers used as predicate adjectives, as in the following sentences: **This final climb was *torture*;** **The horizon kept *shifting, tilting, dropping*; I was *dizzy, nauseous, terrified, certain.*** The other 19 adjectives include articles and modifiers that occur in their more typical spots – before the noun.

Modifier manoeuvres

In your opinion, what is the most important characteristic that a person must have to be successful in life? For example, is it honesty, intelligence, a sense of humour, determination? Perhaps you are who you are because of people who have influenced you – or you've been inspired by stories about others' struggles and triumphs. Without being limited to the examples listed above, write a paragraph. Include proof of your definition of success and write specific examples to explain your answer using predicate adjectives, as well as other modifiers. Remember what we know about linking verbs and predicate adjectives; your sentences are likely to have statements similar to these: 'my dad is honest', 'my aunt seems concerned' and 'I am determined'.

COMPARING AND COMPOUNDING

Adjectives are used not only to describe but also to compare how similar or different two or more nouns are. An adjective has three degrees of comparison: positive, comparative and superlative. For an adjective such as *busy*, the three degrees would look like this: *busy*, *busier* and *busiest*. The positive form is the adjective itself without reference to any other thing, as in '*busy* people'. The comparative degree shows a relationship between two things, to determine which one has more or less value, and is often used with the word *than*. The suffix, or ending, *-er* is used in the regular comparative form with one- and some two-SYLLABLE adjectives, as in 'a *busier* office *than* its competitor'. Adjectives of three or more syllables use the words *more* or *less* as *-er* cannot be added to them: 'a *more realistic* outlook', 'a *less encouraging* viewpoint', 'a *more receptive* attitude'. The superlative adjective demonstrates a relationship amongst at least three things with a positive or negative intensity by using the suffix *-est* or the words *most* or *least* (according to the number of syllables in the adjective). In every case, the determiner *the* is used: '*the biggest* slice', '*the highest* honour', '*the least effective* antidote', '*the most humorous* sketch'.

If the one-syllable adjective ends in a single vowel followed by a single consonant, the final consonant is doubled before adding the suffix, as seen on the previous page with *big/biggest*. If an adjective ends in *y*, change the *y* to *i* before adding *-er* or *-est*, as we have been doing with *busy*, *busier* and *busiest*. Present and past participles used as participial adjectives require the addition of *more/most* and *less/least*: 'a *more exciting* conclusion', 'a *most understanding* committee', 'a *less interested* audience', 'the *least terrified* contestant'. A dictionary is a helpful guide for adjectives with irregular forms whose three degrees are all spelt differently. See Table 1 below for some examples of such adjectives.

The main thing is to not double up on any degree. None of the following is correct: 'the *most beautifulest* ring', 'a *less humbler* person', 'a *more better* option', 'the *most cheapest* price'. Say instead: 'the *most beautiful* ring', 'a *less humble* person', 'a *better* option', 'the *cheapest* price'.

Often misunderstood is the use of *less* for *fewer*. *Less* is the comparative form for a *little* amount, as shown in Table 1. *Fewer* is the comparative of *few*, a small number of individually countable items. If you want *less* stress, head to the express till at a shop, hoping everyone queueing has 10 items or *fewer* in a basket. Consider this television advertisement: **Get more films with *less* adverts!** Each advert can be counted, so the announcer should say, **Get more films with *fewer* adverts!**

COMPARISON OF IRREGULAR ADJECTIVES

POSITIVE	COMPARATIVE	SUPERLATIVE
good	better	best
bad	worse	worst
much	more	most
little (an amount)	less	least

TABLE 1

200

HOUSES THAT ARE 1 YEAR OLD

When a word is already at the highest degree of comparison, it is naturally superlative and cannot be changed to any other degree. Here are some of the adjectives (used in context) that are naturally superlative: *right* turn, *left* shoe, *unique* perspective, *perfect* solution, *original* idea, *fatal* accident, *indelible* ink, *entire* world, *universal* acceptance, *anonymous* gift, *impossible* situation, *eternal* significance, *vertical* hold, *perpetual* motion, *horizontal* line, *dead* battery, *round* ball, *unbelievable* excuse, *final* answer. With these adjectives there are no degrees of variation. Sometimes – but not always – using the adverb *nearly* with a natural superlative is acceptable when making a comparison: a *nearly impossible* situation.

Not all adjectives are one-word modifiers. Adjectives can also be compound, containing two or more words. These PHRASAL ADJECTIVES function as a unit to describe a noun. If used before the noun, phrasal adjectives should be hyphenated to avoid confusing or misinforming the reader. There is a difference between 'a *thought-provoking* argument' and 'a *thought provoking* argument'. The first is a compound adjective that may have initiated a fascinating discussion; the second is a notion that caused a fight to break out. The confusion between the two can be solved with a hyphen. Consider these phrases that all modify *houses*: 1) **two-hundred-year-old houses:** an unknown number of houses that are 200 years old; 2) **two hundred-year-old houses:** 2 houses that are 100 years old; and 3) **two hundred year-old houses:** 200 houses that are 1 year old. Each phrase contains a significant compound modifier but the three examples offer vastly different meanings. Correct placement of hyphens is critical to conveying accurate meaning to readers.

At the very beginning of his short story 'All Gold Canyon' (1905), author Jack London (1876–1916) effectively uses phrasal adjectives to describe a male deer in the canyon's peaceful environment. Look for the six hyphenated phrasal adjectives.

It was the green heart of the canyon... Here all things rested. Even the narrow stream ceased its turbulent downrush long enough to form a quiet pool. Knee-deep in the water, with drooping head and half-shut eyes, drowsed a red-coated, many-antlered buck.

On one side, beginning at the very lip of the pool, was a tiny meadow, a cool, resilient surface of green that extended to the base of the frowning wall. Beyond the pool a gentle slope of earth ran up and up to meet the opposing wall. Fine grass covered the slope – grass that was spangled with flowers, with here and there patches of colour, orange and purple and golden. Below, the canyon was shut in. There was no view. The walls leaned together abruptly and the canyon ended in a chaos of rocks, moss-covered and hidden by a green screen of vines and creepers and boughs of trees. Up the canyon rose far hills and peaks, the big foothills, pine-covered and remote.

The author describes the buck with the following phrasal adjectives: *knee-deep*, *half-shut* eyes, *red-coated*, *many-antlered*. The canyon itself is *moss-covered* and the foothills are *pine-covered*. Each compound modifier contributes to the sharpness of the scene. London could have extensively described the buck that was nearly asleep while standing in the water and the moss on the rocks below the pine trees in the canyon, but his word choices are expanded by the ability to use phrasal adjectives in drawing a grand, majestic picture – and doing so in fewer words.

Any writer can form precise descriptions. However, when using hyphenated compounds extra care is needed as certain English words and phrases seem to go through the stages of first being hyphenated, then to being two words without the hyphen and finally to becoming one compound word. An up-to-date dictionary entry will show the accepted hyphenated phrase but if you can't find it in the dictionary, treat the compound adjective as separately notated words.

KNEE-DEEP
MANY-ANTLERED
HALF-SHUT

BUILD YOUR OWN SENTENCE

To infinity and beyond?

Here's an activity that requires going beyond this page. Refer to Table 1 on page 25 for the comparative and superlative forms of these words: *good, little* and *much*. Then consult a dictionary for the correct spelling of the degrees of these adjectives: *far, fierce, short* and *young*. Pick at least five of those seven adjectives and, using all three degrees (positive, comparative and superlative), write about a situation that goes from bad to worse to worst – or one that comes out for the best. You may choose to be the instigator or the victim of your imaginary plot. Will you barely survive or overwhelmingly triumph?

JUST WHAT IS A PREPOSITION?

Another PART OF SPEECH that has a connection with the people, places and things making up nouns and pronouns is the preposition. A preposition is a word that describes a relationship between other words in a sentence. It is paired with a noun or pronoun that follows a determiner. All of these words together form a prepositional phrase. Here's a test. Pick up this book in one hand. Place your other hand *above*, *on*, *behind*, *under*, *beside*, *beneath*, *against*, *below*, *over*, *by*, *in* and *upon* it. Individually, the prepositions give a direction with the words *the book* being understood. Now follow the instructions of these phrases: put your hand *within* the book, *amongst* the pages and carry it *round* or *across* the room, *towards* the bookcase *for* a while *without* thinking much *about* it.

The prepositions mentioned above explain the relationships *between* you and the book. If you try to define the words by themselves, you'll end up gesturing with your hands or using additional prepositions just to explain your prepositions. Try it. What is *before*? Well, it's just *in* front *of* something, isn't it – as opposed to its being *after*, *behind* or *at the back of* it. And we know *during* means just that, *during*. *Beneath* means *under* – but what does *under* mean? *Below*? Here we go again!

It is no wonder that prepositions are

TO BY

especially confusing for students for whom English is a second language. We say we go *to* school, are *at* school and learn while we are *in* school. When ill we are sent *to* bed to lie *on* or *in* it. For native English speakers, these short words present little difficulty but translating from another language gets complicated. Spanish speakers might say **Why did you do that?** for the more informal English sentence **What did you do that for?** and not understand how the informal translation relates. Even though an English preposition can sometimes appear at the end of a sentence to avoid a clumsy sound, in Spanish there is no corresponding alternate word order.

IN

Another difference lies in a simple and very common preposition such as the Spanish *en*, which can be translated not only as *in* but also as *to*, *by* and *about*, depending upon the context of the sentence, even though Spanish also offers more specific counterparts for each of those words. English has so many more prepositions that don't overlap! Keep a good dictionary close at hand to check individual preposition usage with certain words and check out Table 2 on the next page for a list of commonly used prepositions.

AT OF

Some of the words in Table 2 may also function as adverbs when modifying verbs, as in **Please sit *down*.** But as prepositions they will always have objects. Here's an example: **The driverless car rolled *down the hill*.** Prepositional phrases may characterise nouns and pronouns as adjectives do, answering an adjectival question such as *which?* in phrases like 'the shops *in the centre*'.

ON
UP

PREPOSITIONS

about	above	across	after	against
along	amidst	amongst	around	as
at	before	behind	below	beneath
beside	besides	between	beyond	but (meaning except)
by	concerning	considering	despite	down
during	except	excepting	excluding	for
from	in	in front of	inside	into
like	near	of	off	on
onto	opposite	outside	over	past
per	regarding	round	since	than
through	throughout	to	together with	towards
under	underneath	unlike	until	up
upon	via	with	within	without

TABLE 2

HERE WE GO AGAIN!

While it may be acceptable to end a sentence with a preposition to aid in understanding, it is not always justifiable in formal expression. A stilted conversation might allow **For what are you waiting?** when the informal wording, **What are you waiting *for*?** says what a person wants to know. That use is all right. But asking someone **Where are you going *to*?** or **Where's my book *at*?** is never grammatically acceptable. Instead, say **Where are you going?** and **Where's my book?** Drop the ending preposition. Here are some other unnecessary prepositions that can crop up mid-sentence as well: **The girls met ~~up with~~ their mum at the restaurant;**

Toby jumped off ~~of~~ the deck; Jamie came bounding out ~~of~~ the door.

Where prepositions should be placed in a sentence might sometimes be up for grabs but the traditional usage of the prepositions *between* and *amongst* should be clear. We use *between* in expressions of two objects and *amongst* when talking about three or more. **Drink plenty of water *between* meals** implies the time period separating two meals. This sentence gives an appropriate use of *amongst*: **Divide the chores *amongst* the six of you, so you'll finish cleaning the house by midday.**

Every preposition needs an object to

complete its phrase. Objects are tangible (can be seen or touched) and show relationships to the other words in a sentence, so they function in the OBJECTIVE CASE. In the two examples from the previous paragraph, *meals* is the object of the preposition *between* and *six* is the object of *amongst*. When the object uses pronouns and is compound – using *and* – this can complicate matters. The NOMINATIVE CASE pronouns *I*, *we*, *he*, *she* and *they* are used as subjects but cannot serve as objects. This is true in all cases, not just for *between*; use objective case *me*, *us*, *him*, *her* and *them* with all prepositions. Saying **Just *between* you and *I*** is problematic as the compound object pronouns must both be in the objective case.

As 'I' is in the nominative case, we should say, **Just *between* you and *me*.** It follows then, that you may sit *between him and her* but not *between her and I* or anybody else who isn't an object. Likewise, it's one thing to come *between them and us* but don't ever try it *between they and we* – objects of the preposition *between* must be objective case (*them*, *us*). If you have trouble remembering which pronoun to use, think about the phrase 'between us'. As 'us' is the correct use of the objective case, any other pronoun in that spot – the object of a preposition – will also have to be objective case. Learn which pronouns qualify for that spot and you'll spare yourself a lot of trouble.

BUILD YOUR OWN SENTENCE

Lasting relationships

In prepositional phrases with compound objects joined by 'and', the objective case is needed on both sides of the conjunction. Rewrite the following sentences choosing the correct pronoun from each pair in brackets. Refer to the information on page 37 if you need help deciding which choice is the objective case.

1. WE DIDN'T WANT TO GO HOME
   WITHOUT (HE, HIM) AND (SHE, HER).
2. VIC SAT BEHIND CAROL AND (I, ME).
3. EVERYONE WAS THERE EXCEPT
   LEE AND (HER, SHE).
4. JUST BETWEEN YOU AND (I, ME), I
   THINK SID WAS RIGHT.
5. WILL YOU COME WITH (HE, HIM)
   AND (ME, I)?
6. THE VAN STOPPED JUST NEXT TO
   (THEY, THEM) AND (US, WE).
7. THAT COULD EASILY BE DONE BY
   (HER, SHE) AND (I, ME).
8. EVERYONE GATHERED AROUND
   (HE, HIM) AND (SHE, HER).

ANSWER KEY

1. him, her; 2. me; 3. her; 4. me; 5. him, me; 6. them, us; 7. her, me; 8. him, her.

SIGNIFICANT SIDEKICKS

Prepositions are sometimes so firmly connected to other words in an expression that they almost sound like one word. This can happen with many adjectives and prepositions that, when used together take on a certain meaning, as in **I am so *excited about* it!** Remembering what you know about linking verbs (*am*) and the predicate adjectives that follow them (*excited*) to describe the subject (*I*), as well as what you know about prepositions (*about*) and their objects (*it*), you can readily see how *excited* and *about* go together. In each cell of Table 3, the first word is an adjective and the second word is a preposition. See how many word pairs sound familiar.

If you're not *accustomed to* thinking about adjective-preposition phrases, you may be *doubtful of* the concept and even *surprised by*

ADJECTIVES WITH PREPOSITIONS

accused of	accustomed to	acquainted with	addicted to	afraid of
allergic to	amazed by	angry about/with	annoyed with	answerable to
anxious about	ashamed of	attached to	aware of	based on
capable of	careful with	conscious of	delighted about	dependent upon
different from	doubtful of	excited about	faithful to	familiar with
famous for	fond of	good at/for/with	grateful for	guilty of
happy about/for	identical with/to	interested in	jealous of	limited to
nervous about	opposed to	pleased with	popular with	proud of
ready for	related to	responsible for	satisfied with	serious about
similar to	sorry about/for	suitable for	sure of	surprised by
suspicious of	tired of	typical of	unaware of	worried about

TABLE 3

the number of pairs of words in the table. But after looking at them you'll be *satisfied with* the idea, rather than *suspicious of* it, because – as you can see – many predicate adjectives are *dependent upon* prepositions and they're *good for* each other. Be *pleased about* learning something new!

Connecting words to make a particular relationship requires an understanding of the preposition, the object and the total effect on the sentence. See how many of the 20 prepositional phrases (a group of words beginning with a preposition and ending with its object) you can identify in the following excerpt of *Italian Byways* (1883) by English author John Addington Symonds (1840–93). Refer to Table 2 on page 35 if you get confused. Here's a hint: there are 14 different prepositions used.

The night was pitchy dark and blazing flashes of lightning showed a white ascending road at intervals. Rain rushed in torrents, splashing against the carriage wheels, which moved uneasily as though they could but scarcely stem the river that swept down upon them. Far away above us to the left, was one light on a hill, which never seemed to get any nearer. We could see nothing but a chasm of blackness below us on one side, edged with ghostly olive trees, and a high bank on the other. Sometimes a star swam out of the drifting clouds; but then the rain hissed down again and the flashes came in floods of livid light, illuminating the eternal olives and the cypresses which looked like huge black spectres [ghosts]. It seemed almost impossible for the horses to keep their feet as the mountain road grew ever steeper and the torrent swelled around them. Still they struggled on.

Symonds uses prepositions to mark relationships in acts of nature such as 'flashes of *lightning*' and 'rain rushed in *torrents*', as well as the condition of roadways and wheels, as in 'ascending road *at intervals*', 'splashing *against the carriage wheels*' and 'swept down *upon them*'. He precisely describes the grim destinations as '*above us*', '*to the left*', 'light *on a hill*', 'nothing *but a chasm*', '*of blackness*', '*below us*', '*on one side*', 'edged *with ghostly olive trees*', 'bank *on the other*', 'swam out *of the drifting clouds*', 'came *in floods*', '*of livid light*' and 'looked *like huge black spectres*'. Finally, there are two phrases about the horses: 'almost impossible *for the horses*' and 'torrent swelled *around them*'. Prepositions do not stand alone; they need objects. Words help each other and accurate descriptions are the result. What would have been left without the prepositional phrases? Let's have a look:

The night was pitchy dark and blazing flashes __ showed a white ascending road __. Rain rushed__, splashing __, which moved uneasily as though they could but scarcely stem the river that swept down __. Far away __ __, was one light __, which never seemed to get any nearer. We could see nothing __ __ __ __, edged __, and a high bank __. Sometimes a star swam out __; but then the rain hissed down again and the flashes came __ __, illuminating the eternal olives and the cypresses which looked __. It seemed almost impossible __ to keep their feet as the mountain road grew ever steeper and the torrent swelled __. Still they struggled on.

Now, what if we also take out all the adjectives? Our 155-word excerpt would be reduced to only 78:

__ night was __ __ and __ flashes __ showed __ __ __ road __. Rain rushed__, splashing __, which moved uneasily as though they could but scarcely stem __ river that swept down __. Far away __ __, was __ light __, which never seemed to get any nearer. We could see nothing __ __ __ __, edged __, and __ __ bank __. Sometimes __ star swam out __; but then __ rain hissed down again, and __ flashes came __ __, illuminating __ __ olives and __ cypresses which looked __. It seemed almost __ __ to keep __ feet as __ mountain road grew ever __ and __ torrent swelled __. Still they struggled on.

What a struggle writing would be as well, if we had no adjectives and prepositional phrases! Modifying, describing, characterising, changing, enhancing: that's what adjectives and prepositions do as they form relationships with other words in their sentences. Precisely answering *what kind? which?* and *how many?* can guarantee that the adjectives you throw will stick to your nouns – and in your readers' minds – just as your correctly constructed prepositional phrases can also do. A writer's dedication to exact expression determines how effective he or she is in communicating specific thoughts and ideas. Be accurate, say what you mean and stick with it!

BUILD YOUR OWN SENTENCE
Phrasal focus

Phrases are groups of words that have one function. Prepositional phrases begin with a preposition (Table 2, page 35) and have a noun or pronoun object; adjective-preposition phrases (Table 3, page 41) include a modifier as well. See what combinations you can form by writing your reaction to the following statement: 'Television has destroyed communication amongst friends and family.' Examples from your own experience will be your strongest defence of your position. Write with authority – whether you are opposed to the statement or not. For practice in identifying prepositional phrases, reread this activity's description; each sentence has at least one prepositional phrase in it.

GLOSSARY

common: a class of nouns or adjectives, rather than a particular one such as a *country* (common noun) and a *foreign* country (common adjective with a noun)

complete predicate: the part of a sentence that contains the verb and any modifiers that complete the sentence

complete subject: the part of a sentence that contains a noun or pronoun and any modifiers that describe it and help complete the meaning of the subject

connotation: the suggested or implied meaning of a word through the associations it brings to the reader's mind

irregular form: not the regular structure; the entire word may change, as in irregular verb tense forms (*speak*, *spoke*, *spoken*) and irregular forms for comparative and superlative degrees of adjectives and adverbs (*well*, *better*, *best*)

linking verb: a verb that does not have action; it joins the subject to its complement

modifiers: words or groups of words that describe, limit or qualify another word

nominative case: the classification of nouns and pronouns that function as subjects and predicate nominatives (*I*, *we*, *you*, *he*, *she*, *it*, *they*)

noun phrase: a group of words that includes a noun and its modifiers

objective case: the classification of nouns and pronouns that function as receivers of action or as objects of prepositions (*me*, *us*, *you*, *him*, *her*, *it*, *them*)

part of speech: the class or category into which a word may be grouped according to its form changes and its grammatical function; in English, the main parts of speech are verbs, nouns, pronouns, adjectives, adverbs, prepositions, conjunctions and interjections

phrasal adjectives: compound modifiers of more than one word that function as a unit to describe a noun or a pronoun; they may be hyphenated

proper: a classification of nouns or adjectives that are capitalised, designating a specific one, such as the country of *Uganda* (proper noun) and an *African* country (proper adjective with a noun)

punctuation: marks used to provide meaning and separate elements within sentences, such as full stops, commas, question marks, exclamation marks, semicolons, colons, hyphens and brackets (parentheses)

sentence: a unit of expression that contains a subject and a verb and expresses a complete, independent thought

syllable: a unit of pronunciation having one vowel sound, with or without surrounding consonants, forming the whole or a part of a word

thesaurus: a dictionary of synonyms, or words that mean exactly or nearly the same as other words

RESOURCES

Eats, Shoots & Leaves: The Zero Tolerance Approach to Punctuation by Lynne Truss, Profile Books/Fourth Estate, 2003/2009

My Grammar and I (or should that be 'Me'?): Old-School Ways to Sharpen your English by Caroline Taggart and J A Wines, Michael O'Mara Books, 2008

New Hart's Rules: the Handbook of Style for Writers and Editors adapted by R M Ritter from Horace Hart's original book, Oxford University Press, 2005

Oxford A-Z of Grammar and Punctuation by John Seely, Oxford University Press, 2009

Oxford English Thesaurus for Schools by Susan Rennie and John Mannion, Oxford University Press, 2010

For online punctuation lessons, go to: *www.grammar-monster.com/*

This BBC website has several games for learning punctuation: *www.bbc.co.uk/schools/ks2bitesize/english/spelling_grammar/*

INDEX

adjective classes 14
   common 14
   proper 14
adjective degrees of comparison 24–25, 26, 30
   comparative 24, 25, 30
   irregular 25
   less and *fewer* 25
   positive adjectives 24, 25, 30
   superlative 24, 25, 26, 30
   and word endings 24–25
adjective placement 6
adjectives and questions answered about nouns and
       pronouns 9, 11, 12, 43
adverbs 34
articles 17–18, 20, 32
   and consonant sounds 17, 18
   and noun phrases 17
   and vowel sounds 17–18
Avi 18–19, 20
   The True Confessions of Charlotte Doyle 18–19, 20

conjunctions 38
Cooper, James Fenimore 15–16, 17
   The Last of the Mohicans: A Narrative of 1757
       15–16, 17

Herriot, James 6–8, 9
   The Lord God Made Them All 6–8, 9

London, Jack 26–27, 29
   'All Gold Canyon' 26–27, 29

Norris, Frank 9–10
   The Octopus: A California Story 9–10
nouns 4, 5, 6, 9, 11, 12, 14, 15, 17, 18, 20, 26, 32,
       43, 44
   common 14
   count 17
   proper 14, 17

objects 34, 36–37, 38, 40, 41, 43, 44
   compound 37, 38
   in the objective case 37
over-used adjectives 11, 12

pairs of adjectives and prepositions 40, 41
participial adjectives 14–15, 17, 25
phrasal adjectives 26, 29
predicate adjectives 18, 20, 23, 40
prepositional phrases 5, 32, 34, 38, 40, 43, 44
prepositions 4, 5, 32, 34, 35, 36, 37, 40, 41, 43
   ending sentences 34, 36
   in Spanish 34
   table of 35
   unnecessary 36
   and usage 34, 36, 37, 43
      between and *amongst* 36, 37
pronouns 4, 5, 6, 11, 12, 18, 32, 34, 37, 38, 44
   in the nominative case 37
   in the objective case 37, 38
punctuation 4

subjects 11, 18, 20, 37, 40
Symonds, John Addington 41–42, 43
   Italian Byways 41–42, 43

thesauri 6

verbs 6, 11, 14–15, 17, 18, 20, 23, 34, 40
   linking 18, 20, 23, 40
   see also participial adjectives